All Sorts of Things and Weather
and
A Familiar Compound
Ghost Reconstituted

Compliments of:
Estate of Janet Piper
P.O. Box 474
Huntsville, TX 77342-0474

All Sorts of Things and Weather

and

A Familiar Compound Ghost Reconstituted

by
Janet Piper

Table of Contents

INTRODUCTION

Janet Piper's poetry gives ample evidence of great powers of observation and enormous concern for the social, theological and political welfare of her fellow men and women. No major political system, no important social context or consequence, and no significant theological aim or controversy escaped her attention. She watched and listened to the debates in all these fields, and her poetry is filled with penetrating insights which have one great philosophical center. That is, she was on the side of freedom of thought and action for every individual, and she resented and reacted sharply against any law, doctrine, social arrangement or educational program which limited or curtailed the freedom of the individual to act upon informed convictions and acute moral principles.

The two portions of the present volume offer numerous examples of Piper's wide-ranging reactions to the tyrannies of the mind. In the first section, one finds reflections on men and women, money, political manipulations by the powerful, the dangers of depending upon the past as a guide for present-day action, and, most importantly, the folly of an unexamined bondage to religion and religious leaders.

The emphasis Piper places on religious tyranny was of special concern to her. She found it difficult to accept that supposedly intelligent and well-educated people seemed to believe religion should not be scrutinized with the same skeptical eye they would cast upon other fields of human activity. Since she believed that there is no empirical evidence of the truth of religion, and since she was so well-acquainted with the long, hideous and sorry history of religious persecution, she found it dangerous and inexcusable that so many people saw religion as a taboo area for inquiry. Seeing otherwise rational people become so gullible appalled her, and she recognized that the devious and consciously manipulative actions of religious leaders succeeded because they were not subjected to full examination.

In short, Piper's great philosophical aversion was to control over the minds of men and women, and, as she did with religion, she also set out to reveal how literature, and specifically modern literature, obscures its true purposes in an effort to clandestinely steer its readers toward the social, political and theological positions its authors espouse.

The second major portion of the present volume is a poetic delineation of the dark motives in modern literature — the attempt to re-establish an hierarchical society based on faith and aristocratic values that would be hospitable not to the common man but rather to a self-appointed and self-congratulatory elite.

Piper details the Aiken-Eliot-Pound conspiracy to reassert classical and aristocratic values in literature and to denigrate and destroy the Romantic literary ascendancy that had held sway through much of the nineteenth century. She also notes with profound distaste the support given to dictatorial and royalist regimes by modern literary figures, and she reveals the startlingly ugly disregard for the common man that is a theme or thesis of so much modern literature and art. Her purpose is to make the strategies of modern literature known to as wide a public as possible, and she believes that in so doing she will make a major contribution to the maintenance of freedom both in thought and in politics.

Thus, the perceptive reader of Janet Piper's poetry, both in this volume and elsewhere, should always remember her major premises and abiding concerns. She loved freedom of mind and body, and she longed for a day when her fellow citizens of the nation and the world would throw off the ancient manacles of the mind that have been imposed upon them in all societies. Piper was a child of the Enlightenment, and, although she recognized their severe limitations, she believed reason and scientific inquiry are the only tools we have to try to unravel the mysteries of human existence. They will help us to clear away the crippling inheritances of superstition and irrationality that so far have doomed most men and women to lives of mental, social and theological servitude.

Piper set a great challenge for herself. This and other volumes of her poetry constitute an heroic attempt to extend the inestimable benefits of mental freedom to all her fellow human beings. She loved and pitied mankind, and she gave her life to the betterment of all who would heed her message.

Dr. David S. Gallant
December, 2006

All Sorts of Things and Weather

Men, Women and Money

Men

THE MEASURE OF MAN
(According to the Media)

1

Ambition — competition — acquisition —
    Who won which prize?
Money, money, money!
    How much are they worth?

What kind of car
    Does he drive?
What socialite, model, actress
    Has he taken to wive?

How many mistresses does he —
    How many lovers does she — have?
Money, money, money!
    Will there be palimony?

Whom will they next
    Bag for spouse?
What current celebrities
    Frequent their house?

2

What do they know about Rights —
    (Or right?) Of men? Of Women?
Of Blacks, Reds, Yellows or Whites?
    What will they fight for? And when?

If there is change,
　　　　Will it be for the better?
If they win or lose,
　　　　Does it matter?

MISANTHROPIST

I used to view Robinson Jeffers
　　　　As a Neanderthal, a monster —
Reading of his work with horror —
　　　　And revulsion – tales of murder
And incest-spawn of a sick mind-A misanthropist,
　　　　In need of an analyst.

I supposed that with age
　　　　I had grown tolerant —
Increased in compassion.
　　　　Today I am shocked to find
My changing mind
　　　　Has changed in reverse direction.

What hope can there be for man
　　　　Who is, after all,
An animal, a natural
　　　　Predator — dangerous,
Unpredictable, carnivorous?

THE MALE OF THE SPECIES

1

They are a loutish, brutish,
      Unprepossessing lot,
When not
      Positively frightening,

I avoid them all
      As much as I can;
Lawyer, doctor, plumber,
      Businessman.

To see them on television
      Is close enough;
The better they are
      The farther off.

2

David Attenborough,
      John Kenneth Galbraith —
From time to time
      Renew my faith.

WOMEN

THE WOMAN QUESTION

Jonathan Swift, it is said,
      Expressed this opinion:
"A very little wit is valued in a woman
      As we are pleased by a few words
Spoken by a parrot."

What did Stella or Vanessa
      Think of this judgment?
Did they contradict the verdict,
      Worship, fully assent?
Or simply feel sorry

For the crusty old Tory?
      Before he died,
Savage, senile, and mad,
      He bemoaned the "genius"
He "once had."

"NOW!"—AND THEN?

1

My feminist friend
    Priding herself on her sophistication,
Recoils in horror at the mention
    Of atheism, or even agnosticism.

Equality between the sexes,
    Toleration in sexual mores,
Are the only changes required
    To achieve what should be desired.

2

When women have power to corrupt
    And be corrupted — equal to men,
All will be well on earth
    As it is in heaven.

"WOMEN, BEWARE WOMEN!"

How did we women
        Become what we are?
Who knows?

Our secret, as dark
        As that of the men,
Is open to speculation;

Almost anything goes —
        As the thesis of these
Books reviewed,

Abundantly shows.
        Mrs. Blaffer Hardy's points
Are well-taken,

But will hardly make news;
        No feminine faiths
Will be shaken.

We have always known
        There are wicked witches
One must beware of,

And that bearers of feminine graces,
        Wearers of pretty faces,
Do not always,

And everywhere,
        Inspire devotion
And love.

MONEY

MONEY: PAEAN IN PRAISE

I am at fault to speak
      Less than respectfully
Of Money.

In Age, I owe it
      What I have
Of Comfort and Dignity.

Neither my virtues
      Nor talents —
Such as they are —,

My "advanced" Education,
      Nor past
"Honorable" employment.

Would insure
      My Middle Class status
As tax-paying citizen,

Nor save
      Me from the equivalent
Of Poor-House and Pauper's grave;

That is, shelter of the Streets,
      And a slab in the lab
At the morgue.

• • •

Money can!
      I lift my voice
In Praise and thanksgiving,

If not for Life,
      For an
Endurable Living.

MONEY

1

I have pledged my faith
    To John Kenneth Galbraith,
My favorite Scotsman;
    A soft touch
For anything Scotch,
    I am his exuberant fan.

I admire his books
    And am awed by his looks;
More than life-size,
    His craggy features
Would enhance Mt. Rushmore —
    I am content to adore.

He knows all about money —
    The sacred theme
Of the Reagan regime,
    And its hegemony.
How to invest it – save it – spend it
    But, above all, how to get it.

By hook, crook, or politics,
    Sound or phony,
Pats on the back, or a few licks
    To the boots of a crony:
Tips from loyal insiders
    Or lucky supply-siders.

MONEY

2

When I was young,
    A million dollars
Was a lot of money;
    A man who "made" it
Was a millionaire —
    And lucky.

Looked up to with admiration
    And awe — less of the former than
The latter, I guess.
    He had achieved "Success",
He was the great American showpiece —
    Energetic and plucky.

A million dollars today,
    Is peanuts, small potatoes,
Private fortunes, it seems,
    Are now reckoned in billions;
The national debt, but not the G.N.P.,
    In trillions.

MONEY
3

Money isn't everything —
    It won't buy love,
Or friendship, or filial devotion.
    No, but it will
Further their acquisition.

Try acquiring these
    Without it – and envision
Your lonely sad end,
    <u>Sans</u> love: <u>sans</u> comfort of offspring,
Or kinsfolk; <u>sans</u> friend.

MONEY
(For Arnie Levin)

"Just count it out, Henderson - - don't fondle it"
<u>The New Yorker</u>

I can't handle it,
      Much less fondle it;
I am afraid of the stuff,
      But believe I have enough
To live on —
      If I don't last too long.

FREEDOM OF SPEECH
AND
OTHER FREEDOMS

FREE SPEECH

Everyone has the right
    To say what he thinks —
To speak his conviction
    Without inhibition,

Not, of course
    Without restriction
Leading to loss of freedom,
    Or worse.

If restrained, however,
    By doubt or diffidence,
He merits confidence,
    Shows good sense.

In eschewing
    His strong,
Inalienable right
    To be wrong.

The Free Society
(For Lady Liberty – Honoring Her Birthday)

1

In this Society to have a thought
        Differing from that
Of the ostensible majority —
        A violation of Consensus and Conformity —
Is not simply to be looked at askance,
        Receive a hostile glance,
But overwhelming defeat;
        To face the threat
Of isolation —
        "Excommunication" —
Perhaps "durance vile."

Supposing I were to say:
        "I think Russia is better off
Under the Soviets
        Than under the Romanoff
Dynasty; I don't believe the forces of evil
        Have their locus there,
Though I do not know where,
        I'm sure that the devil
Can work as well
        In Capitalist U.S.A.,
As in Communist Russia — or Hell"!
                (Just supposing!)

2

Supposing I were to say:
        "National television news
Ought to be financed
        Some other way.
Only a fool or complete nitwit
        Would tamely submit
To interruption of attention
        At five-minute intervals —
Or sit through the assault
        Of stupid and/or wicked,
Tasteless Commercials."
                        (Just supposing!)

Supposing I were to quote
        The phrase, "vicious ignoramus"
Or "the one with the silly grin"
        From Christopher Hitchens' two-nation column,
Whom would you
        Guess it referred to?
Ronald Reagan? "Oh, No"!
        Would come the reply;
"He is our President,
        A former movie actor,
And a really nice guy!"
                        (Just supposing!)

LIBERTY WEEKEND: A CLASSICAL MUSIC SALUTE
(Hosts: Kirk Douglas and Angela Lansbury)

I am no Movie Actor's Fan,
But, tonight, I admire Kirk Douglas, the man,

Angela Lansbury's dress
Is a unanimous spectacular success.

I cannot over praise
The gift to us of the <u>Marseillaise.</u>

I have perversely preferred,
Been more profoundly stirred

By the blood-thirsty, "<u>Allons, Enfants de la Patrie</u>"
Than by, "Oh Say can you see?"

Though I have never heard our national anthem sung
More effectively than in the no-longer-young,

Magnificently male, strong baritone
Of Sherrill Milnes, relatively unknown

To me, preferring Pavarotti to Placido Domingo,
 I concede that the latter provides a good show.

Though no opera <u>aficionado</u> or "buff",
I found Leona Mitchell's "Butterfly" moving enough

To evoke nostalgia, if no tears —
The entire program worth its three cheers.

FREEDOM TO CREATE

"Unaffrighted by the silence round them,
Undistracted by the sights they see,
These demand not that the things without them
Yield them love, amusement, sympathy.

• • •

"Bounded by themselves and unregardful
In what state God's other works may be,
Resolve to be thyself, and know that he
Who finds himself, loses his misery."
                    From "Self Dependence"
                    Matthew Arnold

I cannot boast
        Of being "Unaffrighted",
Even "undistracted."
        I have neither hoped
Nor expected

To receive sympathy;
        Much less, amusement;
Least of all, love,
        Resigned, I have gradually

Relinquished all thought
        Of obtaining
A fair hearing, gaining
        Fit audience.

Have I achieved independence?
        These books bear witness
To what degree
        I may claim Victory.

REPRIEVE

1

That involuntary servitude
    Is slavery
I can testify,
    Having mortgaged my maturity
To necessity.

Old Age and Infirmity
    Are not, it may be,
A high price to pay
    For that first taste of liberty,
Freedom from Drudgery.

2

Unfettered Mind is required
    To become "inspired",
Transfer to paper
    Ideas and impressions
In rhyme and meter.

If the result is not
    Immortal verse,
It is at least a reprieve
    From slave labor
And Adam's curse.

FREEDOM OF RELIGION

FALWELL'S NEW NAME

The "Moral Majority" has undergone
    A name change.
I take this to mean
    That Falwell's followers
No longer claim to be
    Either "moral" or a "majority" —
A reversal with which we agree.

The new name their leader
    Has bestowed upon them
Is a different matter:
    The key word, of course, is "Liberty;
Like the words "Freedom" and Democracy"
    It has multiple meanings.
And a dubious history.

"Liberty League", "Liberty or Death Committee",
    "Liberty Network," "Liberty Bell",
and the "White Power Report" —
    "Liberty Bell Press", "Liberty Bell Books"
Willis Cato's "Liberty Lobby";
    Murray Waas runs the list through
In a <u>New Republic</u> article by way of review.

"ACCORDING TO THE SCRIPTURES"

"Born-again Christians"
        Increase, multiply, and may
"Inherit the earth" any day —

An outcome we advocate
        As their fitting fate,
One they richly deserve,

But which, it seems,
        They anticipate
With some reserve.

REVEREND ROBERTSON AND
MR. BUCKLEY AT YALE

Reverend Pat Robertson
        Proudly advertises his law degree
From Yale, where, according to William F. Buckley,

God and Man
        Cohabit, if at all,
"Catch as Catch Can."

Nevertheless, for all Buckley's protests,
        Both Catholics and Fundamentalists
Appear to do very well as Propagandists.

IRANAMOK, IRANASCAM
(Patrick Buchanan and President Reagan)

I have never seen Patrick Buchanan
    Nor a pit bull dog either,
But I feel it would be hard to tell
    One from the other.

From what I read in the papers
    The pit bull dog is vicious.
Ugly, savage, preternaturally tenacious
    In biting.

From the same source, I conclude
    Buchanan, similarly vicious,
Ugly, tenacious, and rude;
    Puts his teeth in his writing.

POLITICS

PEOPLE VS. PUBLIC

1

The "American People" —
    That mystic Entity
For whose welfare,
    In whose name,
The zealous patriots,
    And the Great Communicator
Profess to speak.

Where are they?
    Where do they hide?
How does one meet them?
    Are these the smirking —
Or screaming-robots,
    The manic manikins.
One sees on the screen?

2

The Great American Public
    Is a different matter.
I have to admit
    I am part of it —
Helpless target
    Of a continuous barrage
Of clatter and chatter.

VOICE OF AMERICA

1

There is a crying need
    In the Reagan Corporate State
For a New or Revised Dictionary,
    If Rulers and Ruled
Are to communicate.

Reagan uses old words with a new meaning;
    That is, according to Orwell's Newspeak —
As "Freedom" and "Democracy"
    For "Aggression" and "Hypocrisy", —
Not to mention "Defense" and "Security."

2

In the New Republic "Notebook",
    For August 4, 1986
The egregious Jeane Kirkpatrick
    Aired her brutal politics:

"The effort to give Carter credit
    For Reagan's successes
Is as bold as a bank robbery
    In broad daylight."

Jean's fondness for Argentine generals,
    And her support of their cause,
Is well documented.
    Here the editor commented:

If Kirkpatrick suggests that government policies
    Were helpful in "Returning"
    Argentina to "Democracy",

As she does, she is as bold,
    We may say,
"As a bank robber in daylight,
    Or on holiday."

COLLABORATORS?

Michail Gorbachev, like Christopher Hitchens before him,
    Has committed <u>lese majeste</u>:
He has called President Reagan, in effect, a liar —

Hitchens has documented his accusation:
    Should Gorbachev wish to make use of it
Hitchens, I'm sure, would have no objection.[1]

[1.] In his column, "Minority Report", Hitchens distinguishes between Reagan's senile blundering and ignorant misinformation, and his outright lies, mentioning in particular, the misrepresentation of his World War II service — in which, incidentally unlike his claim, he wore no uniform.

SOUTH AFRICA

1

The Under Secretary of State
    For South African affairs,
Chester Crocker, was perhaps to be seen
    At his most characteristic
And least prepossessing,
    Confronting Congressman Conyers
On the P.B.S. screen.

With his excessive refinement,
    High-browed, rectangular head,
Trim, tiny moustache
    And blond curly hair,
The contrast was classic —
    Saxon Nordic
<u>Versus</u> African Black.

Ignoring his adversary as if unaware
  Of his existence,
Crocker stressed the "quiet diplomacy"
  Of the Reagan regime
So quiet, it would seem —
  The Public had never heard of it,
Nor of the progress

Crocker claimed they had made
  In reducing the rigors
And crimes of apartheid,
  And its victims —
Invisible, inaudible,
  In the United Nations,
 Or elsewhere.

Indignant and frustrated,
  The Congressman refrained
From calling Crocker
  Hypocrite and liar,
As he would have wished —
  And I should have, too, in his place —
And been less restrained.

• • • •

Today Ronald Reagan spoke out
  For the World to hear,
Declaring the principles
  We ostensibly stand for,
But failed to make clear
  Our policy
Of "constructive engagement".

Why today? Through fear?
    Politics, policy?
Diplomacy?
    Demonstration
Throughout the nation
    Has disturbed perhaps, the tenor
Of Crocker's career.

2.

The Afrikaners
    Have staged a coup
Against Bishop Tutu

By the organization
    Of a Black demonstration
Hostile to his omissary.

• • • •

Senator Edward Kennedy —
    Well televised,
And advertised

On the World News,
    With what effect
On viewers and views

Who knows?
    Or those
Of his friends and nephews?

POWERHOUSE

The headline reads: "McFarlane
    Emerges as foreign policy powerhouse",
And the accompanying photograph
    Shows him as I have seen
Him on the television screen —
    Squint-eyed, tight-lipped, mean —
Former lieutenant-colonel, an ex-Marine.

I have just completed an unkind poem
    On Secretary of State, George Schultz,
With the design of "bad mouthing" Haig,
    And less than happy results,
If it elevates and exalts
    A creature like McFarlane, a bad egg,
Lacking even the specious glamour of Haig.

A vicious, humorless man, McFarlane —
    Whether in praise of Botha or the Contras,
In damnation of the Soviets,
    Of Gorbachek and the prospect
Of Summit success.
He clears his speech with no man —
    Even the Secretary of State.

SAILING ON: GEORGE SCHULTZ

1

Given his age and rumored infirmity
      I had thought to extend to George Schultz
The benefit of charity,
      But when I heard him on P.B.S.
Parroting Reagan on Nicaragua
      I changed my mind,
Convinced that he is what he looks like,
      I need not be kind.

Face the facts,
      If there is one thing,
Mr. Schultz lacks,
      It is charisma.

Whether in shorts
      On the tennis courts,
In camera shots
      Embarking or debouching

On planes and ships,
      Or as prime-time speaker
On television,
      He arouses less pity than derision.

Shifty-eyed, dough-faced,
      He affronts the vision
Of watchers, irritates the ear
      Of those who hear

2

His jerky monotone,
    And finish his speech
For – and before – him —
    In sum, pretty grim.

Still, when all is said and done,
    It may be claimed in his favor,
He is not a "loose cannon"
    Like his famed predecessor,

The expansive Mr. Big,
    Alexander M. Haig,
The Would-be Master-in-Charge
    Of the "Ship of State" – or Royal Barge.

He cuts no figure in television,
    Is a good deal less
Than persuasive or glamorous
    And has the grace
To know it. If redeemed he is,
    What redeems him is this:
His devotion to his aging, matronly wife.

Take a hard look at hard-line McFarlane,
    And find, if you can,
One redeeming feature. As the President's spokeman,
    He has no aversion to public life!
Glum, shifty, conceited, crass,
    He meets the illiterate mass
On its own level – to further the cause of evil.

3

Let us salute George Schultz,
　　　　Secretary of State
In his finest hour – late —
　　　　In the Hearing on Contragate.
At last – and none too soon —
　　　　The proper Put-down
Of John Poindexter,
　　　　And that perennial
Adolescent, Oliver North.

We have, however,
　　　　One reservation:
Where does this fracture
　　　　Leave President Reagan?
Both factions profess
　　　　To know him well
And are fanatically loyal;
　　　　Who will venture to factor
The old Movie-Actor?

"POWERHOUSE" REVISITED

We read of the Fall of Princes;
    Today we may watch
On television screens
    The paradigmatic perepeteia
Of once powerful Marines.

Robert McFarlane, groomed,
    Tailored, immaculate,
Returns to the Contra-Hearings,
    As to Life and the Living,
After death and rebirth —

The mouth clamped more tightly,
    The lines on the face deepened greatly,
The voice again resonant and steady,
    Would he prove himself ready
To re-assume place and power?

For glamour, he must rely on his lady —
    Who radiates this to excess —
Has he, perhaps, acquired new virtue,
    New humility, new trustworthiness,
In exchange for "Powerhouse" success?

POEMS FOR THE ATTORNEY GENERAL OF THE UNITED STATES

Of all Calvin Trillin's
　　Uncivil Liberties.
I think I like best
　　His neat and pretty,
Perceptive and witty
　　Piece on Meese.

The motto or logo
　　"Never Indicted!"
Merits more than a laugh.
　　It deserves to be highlighted,
And when Meese goes to his rest
　　May well serve an epitaph.

ODIOUS COMPARISONS

A journalist once took notice
　　That Haig, ousted by Meese,
Was like a giant felled by a midget —
　　I add, or a cipher downing a digit.

After all,
　　Good or bad egg,
Alexander Haig
　　Made the Big League,

To compare him
　　With Edwin Meese Third
Is simply absurd —
　　Like comparing merde with a turd.

THE MEESE COMMISSION ON PORNOGRAPHY

I have clipped the resume
In the <u>New Republic</u> report
And heard the debate on P.B.S.,
But I must confess

What I remember best
Is the famous boast
Of a judge, who claimed
He "knew what it was,

When he saw it," Who does?
Not, it seems, the viewers
Of television commercials,
Late-Nite shows, or even, Prime Time.[1]

---

[1]<u>Traditional Values: Left, Right, and Wrong</u>, an essay by Christopher Lasch, in the first issue of <u>Tikkun: a Quarterly Jewish Critique in Politics, Culture and Society</u>.

SOCIOBIOLOGY

FRATERNITIES, SORORITIES, CLUBS, AND GANGS

Le pauvre enfant ioue
            Avec la boue;
Le riche avec le sable.

I am apprised in the news
            That girls in the inner cities
Have organized themselves into gangs
            As lawless, militant, dangerous,
As those of their brothers.

Bonded, fanatically loyal
            To fellow-members, they wage
Lethal war on all rivals.
            Ranging in age
From twelve to twenty, they swell

The count of the "criminal element",
            Buy, use, abuse, sell
Coke, Speed, Pot, Crack, every drug
            In the traffic – you name it — ,
Indulge in promiscuous sex;

Rob, vandalize, mug —
    Act out the fantasies
Of adolescents depicted
    On scene or screen,
At Rock – and – Roll revels,

Even as, on higher economic levels,
    Their counterparts and peers,
Breaking conventional barriers
    As far as they dare,
Perform their pranks and capers.

SEGMENT – 60 MINUTES

I have reserved space
    For an account of the case
Of Paula Cooper,
    The fifteen year   old murderess
Featured on a segment of "60 Minutes"
    As aired on C.B.S.

I heard the Prosecuting Attorney fulminate
    On the theme of Justice,
And the pragmatic importance of Practice
    In the effect of Lenience on the Juvenile Mind —
And the Judge decree Death, saying there was no choice,
    Given the heinous nature of the Crime.

She had stabbed a pious old lady
    With a butcher knife, not once
But many times, with malice and pleasure,
    While the pious old lady tried to recite
The Lord's Prayer. She was the leader of several other
    High School girls who gained entrance

To the Old Lady's house by the ruse
    That they wanted her "Sunday School Instruction",
Though their motive was robbery,
    But is it not possible that Paula
Instinctively sought to avenge the false promises
    Assured her, in the name of the Christian religion?

What, indeed, were her emotions
    As she plunged the knife in her victim
With no more compassion
    Than primitive women might feel
In slitting the throat of a hog,
    Or disemboweling a chicken.

I viewed the tear-wet face
    Of the fifteen year-old
Bearing still its trace of baby grace,
    While I heard the reporter unfold
The grim facts of her sordid
    But, by no means, exceptional history.

There are nearly a hundred, we are told,
    Juvenile criminals on death row
Whom Paula will join now,
    To prove what? As the Prosecuting Attorney would say,
To like-minded Juveniles, that Justice prevails,
    And Crime doesn't pay!

VIGNETTE

Among the tidbits about the Iran Arms Scandal,
      And the transfer of funds to the Contras —
Government Personnel, and members
      Of Investigating Committees;
Stock Market fraud, chemical leaks,
      Air disasters, riots, and explosions;
The usual toll of local drug violation,
      Rape, arson, and murder;
One item caught my attention

A twenty-two year-old mother had been jailed
      For "child abuse" having failed
To provide a "sitter" for her little girls, aged two, three
      And five-months, left all night alone.
The baby, its wrist gnawed to the bone
      By rats, its face bitten, remained hospitalized,
The older children, though bearing marks of attack,
      Had been able to fend off the predators,
And were now in foster homes.

A week or so later, among other news,
      The Public learned of the release of the mother,
Who had spent the fated night with a "boy-friend",
      And now returned to spend Christmas
With her children and the rats, in their hovel —
      Until she fared forth again
To spend "nights out" and earn
      Subsistence for continued existence
For children and "home".

STATELY HOMES

Why try to make sense
    Of the changing scene
On the television screen —

The castles, halls,
    Parks and belvederes
Of the British peers,

With their collected,
    Or inherited
Objets d'art,

Preceded and followed
    By the sordid and squalid,
Freaked-out London Young?

Thatcher and Reagan, those loving chums,
    Gloat over missiles and atom bombs.
Fund the mansions, ignore the slums;

Reagan calls this "Democratic Capitalism";
    "Caring Capitalism" is Thatcher's late euphemism
For a crude and callous cynicism.

STREET PEOPLE

Some "street people", it would seem,
      Would rather trust their fate,
To the hostility of the Elements
      Than to that of their Fellow-Men.

When the Authorities
      Would gather them into a shelter,
Lest, in sub-zero temperatures,
      They should freeze,

Giving the City a bad name,
      They assert their First Amendment Rights,
And refuse, with the excuse
      They fear robbery and mayhem within.

They prefer to hug gratings
      Over cellars which emit heat,
Or huddle in public lavatories,
      Or doorways in the street,

Fearing less their habitual enemies,
      The cops, than other citizens,
Rendered Savage
      By Deprivation and Rage.

THE INDISSOLUBLE BOND

1

One is loath to listen to news —
    And yet one does
From habit or duty
    As part of society,
Which, reluctantly,

One must be,
    Even at age eight-two
Wholly or partly —
    Beneficiary,
Participant.

As such, one accepts
    One's share
Of the shame and sorrow
    Disseminated there.

2

I am affected currently —
    Haunted nearly —
By the fate
    Of the parents
Of the adolescent youth

Who presumptively
    Sexually assaulted
And murdered a girl
Mail carrier.
In their neighborhood.

II

Jailed and exiled
    For refusing to testify
Against their child
Separated from him and each other,
Now they must suffer!

Why? What crime
    Have they committed?
They have engendered a life - -
    Flesh of their flesh,
Bone of their bone - -

What does it mean?
    Hostage to fortune,
Must one atone
    For what one's children
Have done?

Just? Unjust?
    What is Justice?[1]
It has no place
    In such case.
This bond

None freely repudiates,
    It antedates
All law, legal or moral,
    Saving only
The biological.

---

[1] George Dekker, in *Sailing After Knowledge*, (Routledge and Kegan Paul, London, 1963), page 5, cites Ezra Pound's translation of Confucius' view: "And they said: If a man commits murder Should his father protect him and hide him? An Kung said: He should hide him."

III

MARTYRDOM

Later, I learned
        That Odette Port
Is not the boy's
        Natural mother,

But his stepmother,
        Nullifying thereby
All further speculation
        As to motivation.

She may well
        Regard jail
As preferable
        To the home

Where Father
        And son
Confront
        Their doom.

IV

Today I heard in the news —
    The Grand Jury dismissed,
After four months
    In jail, Odette Port
Had been released,
    And briefly addressed
The local Press.

Her parents, she said,
    Victims of the Holocaust,
Had taughter her
    To hate an Informer;
Especially,
    Never to testify
Against her own family.

The Case, for the present,
    Is closed,
The trial date set.
    One cannot know yet
Its procedure and outcome,
    One is, however, excused,
From further intrusion.

CRIME AND PUNISHMENT

V

"Murder is murder:
        He shot the girl;
He has got to die."

The sentence announced
        As "Life Imprisonment"
Might well be pronounced

"Death by prolonged torture" —
        The boy since age three, diabetic,
Alienated, frustrated, neurotic . . .

The David Port they shut in
        Is damned – whoevever comes out can
Be only the wreck, the husk of a man.

And the girl? Moved to ponder
        The case further, I wonder
If Death is not kinder

Than Life would have been.
        Justice? Mercy? Were they not both
Victims of Ignorance, Inexperience, Youth?

Played upon, exploited
        By pressures, inside and out
Unremittingly applied

In an environment
        Manic, chaotic, sated, —
Sex-saturated.

Opportunity, propinquity tempting the boy,
    The girl, several years older,
Venturesome? titillated? coy?

Apparently she had played
    Along with the game,
Entering the house more than once

Before realizing that this play
    Was "for real", serious,
Irrevocable, dangerous,

And attempting to escape
    The sex-maddened boy,
Intent upon rape.

Guns are guiltless-unaccountable —
    The Father's gun rack close by —
"He shot the girl— he has got to die!"

Let psychologists, biologists, sociologists
    Analyze the Crime —
The "Biological Imperative",

The "System", the "Mores" – Auden's "neural itch"—
    Examine cures and causes —
Social, sexual, judicial – which?

TELEVISION

Television is Debasing your Lives

Debasement implies
      Some standard or norm
To descend from.

Did the U.S. have such
      Before television?
Was the Public in touch?

Did it define
      "The American Way"?
Affect American life?

Television is not
      The greatest wonder
God has wrought —

To grow up weird
      Is far from the worst
Result to be feared.

That the American myth
      Should be destroyed,
By celluloid

Is a bit much —
      Can we face the result?
With what fill the Void?

THE WONDERFUL WORLD OF TELEVISION

I
"Lead them into Temptation!"
      the vendors cry.
"Force them to 'covet!' —
      Seduce them to buy!"

I am not seeking a cure
      For any affliction,
Character defect,
      Or addiction.

I do not wish to be prayed
      For, nor am I swayed
By men who whine, rant, or beg,
      In the name of religion.

I take no comfort in
      Conviction of sin,
Or promise of salvation.
      I have neither faith nor hope

In priest, prelate, or pope,
      Psychologist, psychiatrist,
Sage, mage, or magician,
      (Nor much in the licensed physician).

I feel sympathy for
      The pitiful actor
Who earns his – or her – living
      By posturing, grimacing, and grinning

To further the dubious vogue
      Of "free enterprise,"
And capitalism
      Which would plant

Copies of the Decalogue
    In every school room;
Restore voluntary prayer,
    And safely assume

No one will understand,
    Heed, or read them,
And bite the Providential Hand
    They must rely on to feed them.

II

I am not in the market for
    Any kind of motor car
Limousine, run-about, truck,
    Or any make or size.

I do not wish to squander
    More of my means
On expensive machines
    To clean, cook, or launder.

I am loath to consider
    The respective merits
Of cleansers, deodorizers, detergents —
    Paste, liquid, or powder.

I am not fed
    By pictured food,
Raw, canned, or frozen:
    It does me no good.

My thirst is not sated
    By soft drinks or beer,
Tea, fruit juice, or coffee —
    Whole or decaffeinated.

I do not wish to be sold
          Laxatives, ant-acids,
Sovereign remedies
          For itches, scratches,

Wrinkles, blotches,
          And other defects
Which prevent my attracting
          The opposite sex.

I am immune to the lure
          Of soaps, scents, dentrifices
And other devices
          To effect their capture.

Is this nihilism?
          Am I a nihilist?
No, I am simply tired
          Of being button-holed,

Coaxed and cajoled,
          To buy everything sold,
I am moved to rebel
          Against both hard and soft sell.

I call this "conservative pessimism."
          I do not consider
Myself a Reganite Economist —
          Certainly not a "Supply-sider".

III

Evangelists on television
    And this Moral Administration
Conduct a crusade
    To bully and persuade
The suffering masses to trade
    The intoxication of religion,
The opium of salvation—
    For heroin and sin.

Meanwhile the terminally ill
    Plead in vain
For the drug to ease the pain
    Of "translation" – (dying, that is),
Preferring a temporary euphoria
    To a promissory <u>gloria,</u>
As the living, an actual "high"
    To illusory "pie in the sky."

IV

Judging by the faces
    Of the crowds on the screen
With their applause and grimaces
    They would seem to succeed.

Perennial dupes of defeated hopes
    The starving feed
On the husks they are offered
    For profit and greed,

It is not that one hopes
    To lessen affliction
By drug addiction,
    Power of preachers and popes,

Incorporate in Church
    And State, create
Dependencies,
    More to be dreaded than these.

V.

As if these were not blessing enough,
    We may watch multiple representations
Of a televised Pope
    Resplendent in white drag, (i.e., ritual dress,)
Kneeling to kiss British soil
    (Or is it concrete?)
On the runway
    At the International Airport.

We are permitted to view
    Heads of two Great churches
Anglican and Roman, (i.e. "universal,")
    Meeting to confer
On the enhanced Power
    Which would accrue
To Religion – should they prefer
    To combine them.

THE WONDERFUL WORLD OF TELEVISION
(Houston Weekly)

I tuned in by accident,
    And a little late,
To a program called "Houston Weekly,"
    In the midst
Of a heated debate,

There was a white M.C.
    And a panel of two more —
An uncomfortable youngish librarian,
    And an elderly English professor,
Traditional, correct, authoritarian,

There were, for the rest,
    Perhaps a dozen Blacks —
Men, woman, plus several adolescents,
    Primed to protest
The required reading of <u>Huckleberry Finn,</u>

In an integrated high school English class,
    And to press a request
For its banning,
    These, a reasonable-sounding male parent,
Claimed were the facts:

There were many passages where
    Blacks were referred to
As "niggers", as of "no account",
    As "Deceitful and shiftless",
Even as "less than human."

The beleaguered Academic, taken aback
        By the plain-speaking Black
Patiently, kindly, tried to point out —
        The speakers were really the butt
Of Irony, Sarcasm, Satire,

On the part of Mark Twain.
        His words were worse than wasted
Failed totally of intended effect.
        The Blacks exchanged glances;
The "concerned parent" spoke again.

"That may all be," he said,
        "But these kids don't know that;
They live to-day and what they hear
        Are the insults and slur —
The sniggers of white teachers and classmates."

"It is the Teacher's duty to explain
        The historical precedent
In relation to the present;
        Show it was not meant to be offensive."
So the professor, on the defensive.

A white speaker suggested
        That some black teachers be employed:
Books by black writers be "required".
        A spirited black woman
Seized the floor. Her scorn

Was vitriolic, explosive;
        Her anger cynical, corrosive.
Astonishment flared
        That a black woman dared
Be so frank and outspoken.

"Black teachers! They would never be hired,
        Or if one was, as a token,
Would soon be fired.
        It had happened in Spring, as elsewhere,
When "oil-rich residents ran the School Board."

The words of the professor, shocked, frustrated,
        Grew more heated:
"What about the great Classics —
        Were they to be banned
Because some minority objected?

What about Shakespeare? The <u>Merchant of Venice?</u>
        <u>Othello?</u> Why, in <u>Henry IV,</u> his own ancestors,
The Scots, were maligned.
        Should he mind? Our cultural heritage be depleted
In behalf of the Ignorant and Blind?

In an attempt to defuse
        The contagious acrimony,
The distressed librarian cited
        The Reading Rights of the Many —
Deplored the banning of books.

• • •

I was uncomfortable, too;
        Here was a matter I had long
Given thought to. What good
        Anyway, did "required" reading do
The semi-literate, demoralized Young?

Of those who would "go on" to college,
        (Of blacks very few)
How many would get their "kicks"
        From their "heritage of classics",
Full-scale- or in truncated review?

"Ponies" for English classes now
> Are <u>de riguer</u>,
As once for Latin and Greek;
> Those languages safely buried,
Must we settle for "Newspeak"?

Can we teach "Standard English"?
> Dare we risk "Formal"?
Shall we settle for "Colloquial"?
> For one of several dialects?
For the "Vulgate", "Pidgin", of "Patois"?

So much for the problem
> Of Language – what about Reading?
We can assign titles —
> "Students" can buy Monarch and Cliff Notes —
(And, perhaps, learn to read them) —

It won't do them much harm.
> I will cast my votes
For the Classics (with trots)
> Rather than yield
The bloody field

To Joyce Carol Oates,
> John Irving, Flannery O'Connor,
Science Fictioneers, Sensation-mongers,
> Pornographers, Caricaturists,
Satirists and "Wits".

I would have these youngsters given
> A basic Foundation
For Higher Education
> (If that is possible):
Teach them to read and to write.

Let competent teachers
      Try to teach them what sentence is,
And how to make one —
      How to build these into a paragraph,
And of paragraphs, block by block, make a theme.

Let them have an ample selection
      Of books from easy to difficult, in varying degrees,
On a wide range of subjects,
      To choose from, as they please.
Teach them how to write a book report.

And "require" that they "do," at least, one,
      With careful criticism,
Consultation, and correction.
      Do not prate
To them of "masterpieces,"[1]

Nor of their "cultural heritage." These
      Battles, this warfare — can wait.
Guerilla warfare, on this issue,
      Racial — perhaps, full-scale civil —
Will not.

[1] See "Huck At 100" by Leo Marx, The Nation, August, 31, 1985.

Also "Huckleberry Finn and His Critics" by O. J. Furnas, The American Scholar, (Autumn, 1985).

YEATS' "SECOND COMING" AND TELEVANGELISTS

1

Referring to their "message" and them,
    We may well speak
Of the "Great Beast slouching
    Toward Bethlehem".

The Worst, Yeats said, are filled
    With conviction, passionate and intense —
Television preachers display more evidence
    Of this than good sense.

Schuller is proud of his crystal
    Enormous cathedral;
Falwell is proud of — well,
    Let us say of Jerry Falwell.

2

As for Pat Robertson,
    That one
Is Hell-bent
    On becoming President.

DECISIVE BATTLES

As Gorham Munson long ago,
    And Tim La Haye today, contend —
Exploiting the uncertainties of human-kind —
    The decisive battles of this world
Are those for the popular mind.

Munson, in his <u>Twelve Decisive Battles,</u>
    Analyzes and summarizes
The issues and outcomes
    Of conflict and schism
From the Pagan World to Christendom.

Munson speaks from the point of view
    Of the "Educated", "the Gifted", the "Few";
LaHaye for the fossilized "Moral Majority",
    Brain-bound to a deplorable
Feudalistic religion – or slavery.

ARMAGEDDON

A Houston
Evangelist
       Advertises his
As the religion
       Of "Excitement."

What an Entertainment!
       What greater drawing card
For the anonymous, bored
       Unemployed
Or Wage Slaves
       Than "Jesus Saves"?

But first, the Rest,
       The Damned, the Accursed,
The Sinners, must
       Get theirs – the "Blest"
Win the battle
       Of Armageddon.

Then, having got even,
       Veterans of star wars,
They, as victors,
       Take flight
For an instant
       Hollywood Heaven.

HELL AND DAMNATION

It wasn't until last Sunday
    That I forced myself to listen
To Jimmy Swaggarts' sermon,
    Watch the faces of his audience,
Weigh the fact of his influence
    Judge the force of his "art".

The subject of this program
    Was the reality of hell fire;
The nature of unforgivable sin;
    The certainty of punishment –
And the proportion of the population
    For whom it was meant.

The most faithful and devout
    Individual, or sect,
Could not escape, failing to qualify
    In the one essential respect;
Belief in God and His Son,
    Without reservation or question.

Prayer and self-sacrifice,
    Service to mankind
Will not suffice,
    Even Mother Teresa is destined
To sizzle and burn eternally,
    To mollify heavenly ire.

As I listened to this zealot,
    This half-educated spellbinder,
I could not escape a reminder
    Of Elegant Eliot,
And his consignment of us all,
    To either fire or fire.

YANKEE INTRUDER

A BREED APART

"Salt of the Earth"
  I have called them. So they are!
Salt is an essential seasoning:
  <u>Vide King Lear!</u>

These indomitable Daughters
  Of the American Revolution,
<u>Magna Carta.</u> Republic of Texas,
  Daughters of the Confederacy

Present a formidable redoubt:
  Ancestor – worshipers,
Single-minded, devout;
  Collectors of artifacts.

Legend and anecdote
  Of valiant men
And virtuous women —
  Everyone hero or heroine.

• • • •

Dauntless women,
  Ignorant of their ignorance,
Praising themselves
  In praising them —

Feet firmly planted in reverse,
        Eyes sternly fixed on the Past —
(The very recent past),
        When the reaches of this vast

Continent became theirs by Divine Right;
        That is by invasion, conquest, and theft,
To defend against the aborigines,
        And all later comers —

(Not to be bereft
        From them or their descendants
Forever — theirs in simple fee
        In perpetuity.)

Lot's guilty wife only glanced back,
        And became a by-word, a permanent
Warning — and for punishment.
        Not a soupson, but a pillar of salt!

One accepts with some misgiving
        This militant gestalt —
A regiment of four-square pillars,
        An Army of salt!

PIETAS, DIGNITAS, HUMANITAS

Let the paterfamilias
    Preserve his gravitas
With a straight face —
    If he can.

I find myself unable
    To cope
Even with amour proper.
    As for "Proper pride",

A virtue implied
    In texts on the Humanities,
Who shall decide
    What that is?

As authorities,
    Neither Aristotle
Nor Irving Babbitt, et al.,
    Prove viable.

SYLLOGISMS

Ancestor worship
        For some of my friends
Poses a dilemma.

Taking as premise:
        "I owe my Grandfather
Respect and honor";

Then, "My Grandfather
        Owned slaves" becomes a defense
Of the Indefensible.

• • • •

Our grandfathers accepted
        The Biblical
Myth of Creation;

Does Loyalty constrain
        Us to deny
The evidence of Evolution?

Our ancestors believed
        The Earth was flat;
Must we accept that?

Like all human beings,
        Since or before,
Our forebears were fallible;

Are we, therefore,
        Condemned evermore
To repeat their error?

GARDENING

1

Gardening for pleasure
        Prestige, pastime for leisure —
Is one thing,

Back-breaking toil
        At the behest
Of another,

Whether under the whip
        Or the urge for money —
Altogether other.

Whether on earth,
        In Eden,
Or in Heaven,

I call it Slavery,
        And pronounce it wrong
Wicked, even —

2

No defense, argument,
        Or disguise
Will suffice

To persuade me
        Otherwise,
Though impotent

To effect
        A reversal
Of judgment.

GRUBBING

1

How distinguish
      Between the "Gentleman Planter"
And the "Plain Dirt Farmer"?

Land-grabbers all —
      My forebears in Iowa
Did their own grubbing,

And were, in consequence,
      Grubbier than
The labor-free Planter.

• • • •

My friend cherishes
      An image of her grandfather
(Who died soon after),

Leaning down from the saddle
      On his fine black horse
To address her:

"Little girl, go tell your mother I am here"
      And of herself running
To do his bidding.

2

I remember my weather-beaten
      Uncles in overalls —
Hardy, hearty, and teasing,

Distinguishable from the Planters
      By the sweat
Of their brows

As the latter, by that
      On the brows
Of their Negroes.

TRANSPLANTS

1

Transplanted Iowans —
    Which seemed to me queer —
Were more rabid racists
    Than many born here.

One self-styled "aristocrat",
    Iowa Ph.D., authentic autocrat
Was addicted to anecdotes,
    (Replete with dialectical quotes),

Illustrating Black inferiority
    And White superiority
In magisterial style,
    Designed to beguile

2

His appreciative audience,
    He would recite with delight
How Old Manuel
    Leaning on his rake,[1]

Would "listen-in" with rapt admiration
    On professorial conversation,
How, when reproved, he would
    pick up his rake, and speak,

Offering, with profuse
    Apology, his excuse —
"Ah just loves to hear
    Edyuh-cated folks talk."

[1] Or alternately "broom"

74

TRANSFORMATIONS

1

My friend in the fifties
    Suffered persecution
At the hands of John Birchers
    For her admiration

Of Mrs. Roosevelt and support
    Of the New Deal.
Anguished, she then felt
    The Danger as real.

Later, removed to a larger city,
    Prosperous and complacent,
She gave me an account
    Of her civil activity —

Woman's Club, A.A.U.W., D.R.T. —
    Their membership and programs,
Including a recent meeting of the D.A.R.
    Where "Show and Tell" was the theme.

Each member brought a treasured artifact
    Associated with a great man,
Or some great Event,
    And achievement:

A dish or spoon
    He had eaten from
A ribbon, buckle or button
    From clothes he had worn.

2

Visiting in Jackson, Mississippi,
     Home of Eudora Welty,
And point of origin
     Of the Huntsville Gibbs clan,

She cites the case
     Of the local physician
Summoned by a Yankee newscomer
     To aid in translation

Of a Black patient's description
     Of her "miseries" —
Which he complacently does —
     Proving what? Not

That "We understand our Negroes",
     As my friends supposes,
but as Confession
     Of ancestral guilt

In holding them
     In subjection,
While denying them
     Education.

RESURRECTION

1

Anglo-Saxon migrations
    To Texas, date back
Three or four
    Generations.

Descendants piously preserve
    Artifact and anecdote,
But above all, the ancestral
    Burial plot,

Visited on holidays and anniversaries
    With floral offering and prayer.
To whom? Where?
    To the bones which lie there?

2

Do they believe
    The Inhabitants
Of those graves live —
    Awake and sentient —

Or asleep, awaiting
    Armageddon and the sound
Of Gabriel's trump —
    In the ground;

Swift translation
    To heaven?

They resent prying intent
    As impiety and blasphemy.

On Sunday they say,
    "I believe in the Resurrection of the Dead
And the Life of the World to come";
    Do they?

SELF AND SOCIETY

1

It would appear
    From the attitude
My friends take,
    My views are a mistake;

The experience
    From which I speak —
Eccentric, irrelevant,
    Unique,

To be ignored
    Where possible,
Deplored
    Where not.

2

If I am right,
    What have they got?
What becomes
    Of the Status and Income,

They pride themselves on?
    What of the Image
Of Self and Society —
    They live by?

"BREAD AND BUTTER" LETTER

1

Brain-bound,
      Tradition — shackled,
As they are, I marvel
      There is room
For any virtue to bloom.

These, nevertheless, are multiple,
      In celebration or disaster,
Wedding, christening, funeral,
      Loyalty to friends and above all,
To clan, kin, and kind.

Sometimes even to outsiders
      Of opposing views,
And minimal
      Tact or charm —
Critics of Moral Majority and Supply-Siders,

2

May these bonds of friendship
      Prove as lasting
As those imposed by inheritance!
      Meanwhile, I am grateful
For hospitality and acceptance.

TWO POEMS

1

The ostrich is a redoubtable bird
    With a powerful kick;

It can't fly but is very quick
    On its feet-pronounced, in fact, fleet,

That is, symbolizes regress
    Rather than progress

On the evolutionary scale, is generally accepted.
    It has adequate sight

To use when it chooses;
    It simply refuses

To acknowledge or see
    Facts with which it cannot agree;

2

In this, I think, resembling my friends
    Who bury their heads in the sand,

Rather than revise or bring up to date
    Hand-me-down prejudices they have inherited.

When my friends achieve their ends –
    Catholic, Republican, Evangelical, Tory –

We shall not have a government of peace and riches
    But a consortium of king-like storks and ostriches.

2

It is sad that People
    Not mad, but essentially
Well-meaning and good —
    Keep a bad thing going;

Give artificial respiration
    To sentiments and views that should
Be allowed to die, and would,
    Otherwise, be dying.

If the Daughters and Wives
    Of This, That, and the Other,
However well-meaning or well-meant,
    Would only consent

To let the Dead Past be buried and include
　　　The myriad anonymous lives.
Whose progeny still survives,
　　　Who shared with their own ancestors

The boredom, glory and horrors —
　　　Would open their minds and their eyes
To the roots of current evils and errors,
　　　Corrupt, festering, long-lived,

Would they repent,
　　　Examine and revise
Their celebratory programs,
　　　And priorities?

MEN, WOMEN, AND MICROBES

Or

This Is The Way The World Ends

"THIS IS THE WAY THE WORLD ENDS"

Of "my fellow-Americans" —
    Men or women —
What can I say?

A Mixed Bag – the Lot of them —
    As Individuals,
More of the same.

An excerpt in the <u>New York Times</u>
    From the review
By Melvin Konner —[1]

Of a book, <u>Microcosmos,</u>
By Lyn Margoulis and Dorian Saigan reads:

> ...After we die we return to our forgotten stomp-
> ing ground. The life forms that recycle the sub-
> stances of our bodies Are primarily bacteria. The
> microcosm is still evolving around us and within
> us. You could even say...the microcosm is evolv-
> ing as us.

[1] Melvin Konner, the author of "The Tangled Wing: Biological Constraints of the Human Spirit," teaches anthropology at Emory University.

My own comment
      May be said
To have been anticipated

In a poem
      I wrote
Some years ago:

"Just Fine, Thank You!"

Host of myriad microbes
      Viruses, bacteria,
Without and within,
      I am a territory, a continent,

A firmament, even,
      To colonies of micro-organisms –
Their be-all, end-all, earth and heaven,
      Their armies fight

Like me, day and night,
      For survival, for life —
Less than midge or mite
      In the infinite

• • • •

Could it
      Be thus
God is conscious
      Of us?

THE END OF THE WORLD

Dung and Death!
Dung and Death!

The World Ends
With my last breath.

Only the individual
Fate is final.

A FAMILIAR COMPOUND
GHOST RECONSTITUTED

"A FAMILIAR COMPOUND GHOST" RECONSTITUTED

Let us leave to Dame Helen
And lesser hagiographers
(Or hagiographettes),
To unravel the knots
In the intricate nets
Interwoven so well
In the <u>Works and Days</u>
Of T.S. Eliot —
Theirs be both labor and praise.

I take occasion, however, to demur
At a fulsome review of her
The <u>Composition of "Four Quartets"</u>
By that most deferential of critics,
The eminent Christopher Ricks,
Praising her twenty-six page discussion
Of the most famous passage in "Little Gidding"
(and the most elaborately glossed),
Anent the "familiar compound ghost".

"Great Eliot at his greatest and best"…
"The most humanly substantial and passionately
Chastened passage "…and I quote…
"That T.S. Eliot ever wrote,"
Certainly, not a few
Of his devoted disciples agree.
Russell Kirk says of the "communication of the dead"…
"Time and the Timeless intersect. It has a dread
Grandeur unexcelled elsewhere in Eliot."

Ephebes and epigones have strained every sinew
And brain cell to guess who,
Among the Great of the Past,
Is referred to.
The most favored among the candidates
Is, of course, Dante, (or more recently, Latini).
Russell Kirk adds Swift and Yeats,
Though, in a footnote, he would concur
With Grover Smith's vote for the great Lexicographer.

These awesome names would deter
A less time-hardened character than I am
From reviving a thesis I first advanced
In nineteen hundred and forty-nine,
Expounding the intimate interrelation
Between Eliot and the American poet, Conrad Aiken,
Amounting to identification and bidding
The latter stand and be recognized, without equivocation,
As the famous "Dead Master" of "Little Gidding".

• • •

For anyone who has read with care
The work of both poets in verse and prose,
It should be enough to juxtapose
This passage from Aiken's <u>John Deth.</u>
With that of the encounter in "Little Gidding",
To recognize both poets as "compound ghosts";
The pun "Potter" on Aiken's second name;
As also <u>his</u> <u>leit</u> <u>motifs</u>
Of blowing horn and metal leaves . . .

A Familiar Compound Ghost Reconstituted

By Nanking pool, I saw one ghost
Speak with another; of that host
Mag Oolie knew. — Cried Yuan P'ien;
"Alas — among the dead, again
We meet, old friend! Unresting blown
On the dry wind that whirls on us
To Nowhere out of Nothing! Speak —
Before the wind his hatred wreak
And part our hands!"…Then Hao Shih Chin,

Yet sweet it is 'twixt gust and gust
To pause with you, remembering dust." —
Thus Hao Shih Chin. And Yuan P'ien
Opened sad lips to speak; but then
The long wind blew their hands apart
And whirled their white beards, "Have good heart!"
Each cried to other; and their ghosts
Flew off like leaves with Tao's hosts.

(from <u>John Deth)</u>

I met one walking, loitering and hurried
As if blown towards me like the metal leaves
Before the urban dawn wind unresting…

I caught the look of some dead master
Whom I have known, forgotten, half-recalled
Both one and many; in the brown baked features
The eyes of a familiar compound ghost
Both intimate and unidentifiable…

The day was breaking. In the disfigured street
    He left me, with a kind of valediction
    And faded on the blowing of the horn.

           ("Little Gidding", II, from Four Quartets)

I will not repeat here
What I have said elsewhere
In plain prose: <u>In a Familiar Compound Ghost</u>
<u>Reconstituted</u>: <u>The History of a Lost</u>
<u>Manuscript</u>; in <u>Edwin Ford Piper</u>
<u>And the Iowa Workshop</u>: A Prehistory;
In the rejected "Introduction"
To Mrs. Harris's <u>Aiken Bibliography</u>:
And in miscellaneous verse.

I will eschew
Further citation and documentation
(Which I could amply provide),
Emulating the arrogant dogmatisms
Of the Master and his minions
Obsequious critics — to assert and deride
The duplicity and devious devices
Of the "Modernist" Cult and its devotees —
To confirm and develop my thesis.

The Pound-Eliot-Aiken "fertility rite" or charade
(To be later more fully described)
Constituted merely a sub-unit, as already indicated,
In a much larger counter-revolutionary "brigade"
Centered in France after Napoleon,
Designed to combat the ideas of the French Revolution
And destroy utterly those of the Enlightenment
(Detruire absolument les idees du dix-huitieme siecle)
As the powerful spokesman, Joseph de Maistre, said.

Georg Brandes' Main Currents
In Nineteenth Century Literature
Deals with these ideological wars
And their political corollaries,
In England and on the continent
In several volumes. Many more,
By other authors, corroborate or refute his views
Of that century's conflicts, and scores
Bring the battle to our century and our shores.

In the first decade of this century,
When our young poets were together at Harvard
They were influenced by representatives
Of such an "arriere-garde".
Decked in new dress and various guises,
But embattled and armed to the teeth.
William James's "The Will to Believe"; Irving Babbitt's "Inner Check";
Grandgent, The Dante scholar's Old and New;
George Santayana; Bertrand Russell — to name a distinguished few.

• • •

Not that education was confined
To class-room lectures, academic papers,
Nor even to extra- curricular cliques and capers —
Cynical farcical, dramatic — exploration and experiment
In the powers and purposes of body and mind —
(Yes, even in the possibilities of the Soul),
And always in the meaning and mystery of the Whole
With, for Aiken, besides, minute examination
Of every aspect of a continuing marvelous Creation.

There was also Boston — "restaurants
In gay bohemian poets' haunts
Where poets came with languin locks
And chorus girls in gaudy frocks…"
"Where love was made and money flowing —"
After dinner the long walks,
Idiotic chatter, lofty thought, and endless talks
All to musical accompaniments —
New rhythms and strange instruments.

"Bland horns, drawling trombones"…
The insistent moan of saxophone,
And always the pounding of the drums —
"A tentative perplexing din
Where softly rose a violin
To sing a moving phrase, and then
Was lost in jargonings again . . . "
Crying out "against all that is" . . .
Or breaking the "heart with ecstasies."

Clever students of clever teachers:
Wundt, Freud, and the "new psychology"
To shed light, at last, on man's dark mystery;
New martyrs, old saints — Babbitt's "New Humanism";
German Idealism, via F.H. Bradley — artificial respiration
For old theology; Russell's quasi-atheism;
Santayana's "Realms" and right to "disbelieve"—
Symbolists and Decadents — English and French; —
James's "options" and Will to Believe.

What cosmic design, or fate, or chance,
What mystery of circumstance,
Thrust these gifted youths,
Of contradictory temperament, complementary talents,
Into the common New England soil
To share a natural and social ambience,
Where their symbiotic relationship,
Abundantly nourished,
Grew strong and flourished?

Aiken, precocious and prolific, poured forth
Poems; stories; novels; in tumultuous profusion,
Recording his response to impressions, sensations —
His observations, reflections — questions,
Too, — protests, objections, frustrations —
All to an obligato tuned to the strain
Of season and weather - -elation,
Depression and pain, giving
Short shrift to quotidian living.

Where Aiken pours forth, Eliot reins in;

Where Aiken is garrulous, dense —
Eliot is fastidious, thin
Affecting in outward demeanor
"Correctness" — a decorum maintained
For some fifty years — before
The public was allowed to inspect
Proof of what many had come to suspect —
The dubious character within.

• • •

Of four introductory poems in <u>Earth Triumphant,</u>
Aiken's first book (published in 1914 and for long
Out of print), three, including the title poem,
Are hardly memorable except for the evidence
Of his great and lasting gift; close observation
And lyric transcription of vivid experience
Of a total world of sight, sound and sense;
And — for its time — amazingly frank expression
Of uninhibited, extravagant emotion.

"Romance", "Earth Tedium", even "Earth Triumphant" are tedious,
Trivial, in part; repetitious; but the many invocations
To Earth, defiant, abject; curses, imprecations —-
Groveling, exultant, hating – loving —
Are recognizable; for the most part, convincing,
The sixty-two page paean, "Youth",
As I reread it this morning, moreover, struck me
As more important than I had thought —
Authentic, archetypal, touching, amusing.

Never again would he risk revealing,
With such abandon, his rebellious thought and feeling —
Even here, he superimposes a slight narrative disguise
And, almost as an afterthought, a protagonist (in <u>Youth</u>
Named Jim, but later, in the Symphonies to assume identities,
Multiple, grandiose, portentous — as "Universal Man"),
Henceforth, in essays and appendices,
He would elaborate rationalizations and theories,
To "prove" the value and virtue of what he had done.

Systole, diastole — depressives, manics —
"Il Penseroso", "L'Allegro" (although
Aiken is no young Milton, no John Keats,
Nor even George Byron — rather, a Poe
Filtered through Baudelaire, and back again.)
Influenced by John Masefield and Walt Whitman,
Decadents, Symbolists, neo-Romantics,
Aiken's first poems introduce an American bard,
The Hamlet-<u>cum</u>-Nietzsche of Harvard Yard.

• • • •

Six poems which, with "Dilemma", close the first book,
Polarize the identities, stress the split
Between Eliot-Penseroso and Aiken-Allegro,
Who rejects the pretense that the former represents
Only a phase in his protagonist's own
Life — to be surpassed and outgrown,
As in "Earth Triumphant", where an early sketch
For portraits of Eliot in later poems
And prose — passes for such:

Yet here is given the tale of one
Who took his healing of the sun…
Through all his youth and anchorite
He peered at earth by candle-light,
And on a lamp-lit page would read
Of by-gone times and ancient deed…
And tales in curious language writ,
Strange-charactered by monkish writ,
Ere his own life was yet begun

He had exhausted one by one
Each creed, each weird philosophy,
And reached at last satiety…
He put his books upon their shelf
And went to hear the birds himself,
Threw up the windows, let in sun,
And called philosophising done….
The spring-time of his life was this:
All earth seemed sweet to love and kiss…

And all the universe stood still
While out of love he drank his fill…
And holding love they held the key,
He thought, to immortality…
Lo, beauty like a lightning came…
The man, he mused, who once knows love
No baser lust can ever move;
No, and no human face could lure
His heart again…His earth was sure.

• • •

We have the triumph of a romantic Allegro
Over a not too unattractive Penseroso...
Both reappear in 'Youth", but Aiken-Jim
Is allowed to give free rein to his unabashed sadism,
And like Nietzschaen Superman, to glory
In his god-like beauty and strength, his superiority
To the common herd at Coney Beach,
And the demi-monde of theater, bar
And dance-halls in the city.

• • •

The surf broke whitely along Coney Beach,
But he was sickened by that shrieking crowd....
But he was goaded by that roar of throats,
He hated them, they had no strength, no nerve...
Beauty and strength and youth — he has all these;
He knew his power; he was the purest life,
"Armed with a thirst that glittered like a knife,
A lust for life, for power, a hot clear passion. . .
Knowing that strength was right and weakness wrong...

He was alone, exultant, with the sea,
He had flung earth away, his soul was free...
No hell, no heaven there was, no god or devil,...
By god, he saw it now! There were no laws —
Not one in nature...strength was justice there,
Every heart for itself with teeth and claws..."
The tree-tops burned; he saw the sea-gulls run
Through upper rose-fire, shining, floating free;
They made the most of life, and so would he....

• • •

In the poem, "Romance", Aiken does very well
At divining an inexperienced girl's sexual
Anticipations and response,
As well as a young male's intense
And casual promiscuity.
In "Youth", Jim outdoes Nietzsche
In <u>macho</u> bluster and exuberance:
"He got it (life) by the throat, he was its master;
Sing! went his whip and life danced on the faster:...

> At the stage doors, he met with murmured curses,
> He waltzed the queens away, he had his will;
> He laughed to see the sports look black as hearses
> White-blooded things! Did they have hands to kill?
> He strode, his nostrils quivered stiff with scorn,
> He wondered why these little men were born...
> He danced them out of the world of work and pains,
> Girl after girl, white arms came gladly after,
> The music drew, he danced them off with laughter....
>
> He did not love them — they were shining dust
> Timid and insolent, rotten with fawning lust
> Foolish, with no more depth than peacock's eyes;
> They lusted after him, to make him prize,
> To hold his body or even to take his soul — ...
> Youth yearns to youth, full blood loves full blood only
> He was too bright, too masterful, too keen,
> He was too good for them, so he stood lonely,
> A lonely king waiting the lonely queen...

• • •

Impalpable dream, the warm bright mist of life,
Music, white stars; so dreamed he of a wife....
"A wife? A mistress rather . . . he would not wed:
This was to stoop in chains, renounce his wings,
Break body and heart and soup for daily bread,
Get down and crawl among crawling things!
Life is not life that only day's work brings!
Crush, master, show no mercy, take, not give —
No god save self, that is the way we live...

• • •

Jim, it is true, after a first conversion
To a life of crime, suffers some doubts:
        .... And strangely, then, a doubt came like a flame;
        Was this way life? — he quenched the doubt in wine,
        Walked lightly out...In crowds the harlots came,
        So frank in lust! These creatures knew life's taste,
        They danced it night and day, no hour to waste —
        They danced; — for what was living but a dance?
        Still the same music, though the dancers fade....

        Doubt turned in him...only a moment's space.
        Was life best so? Where was the fight in this?...
But after a time, came renewed misgiving
        What was this life? A laugh, a smutty joke,—
        A drink, a giddy step, a dance, a kiss, —
        Then the long darkness of the last abyss.
        This was not living, but a mad decay,
        Shining in darkness, like all things that rot, —
        A whore-house ball, garish and grim by day....

"Well, he would quit…before his mind's eye passed
A host of things…the Amazon…Tibet—
Africa—There, exploring, he might forget
These effete countries, aswarm with maggot man, —
Masterful, where great winds, great rivers ran—
Honduras, Hayti, —rebellions every day;
He might be king—or fly-blown in a ditch,
Imperial Caesar, dead and turned to clay!…
Turn socialist? Ah, no, it made him itch,…

• • •

Before the escape from sinful Boston,
Jim killed a man and simply ran —
Not to find adventure across the water,
But hard work on a New England farm
Where Jim-Aiken finds again the charm
Of the pastoral life and the pure love
Of the farmer's simple daughter; …
This was life's flower, life meant no more than this!
Body and soul surrendered in one kiss —…

A long while then, leaning on window-sill
Jim stared at night; he felt a great calm spread
Wide in his soul…as if his youth were dead…
As if all strength, all fierceness, lust for life
His love of war, the glittering of the knife, —
Faded, dislimned, all vanished in this hour.
A sadness drooped his spirit…Would he cower,—
Dream life away? Well, maybe dream was best,
Dream, and the long slow years of calm and rest…

No feverish search through the mad universe,
Fighting to crush the small and kill the strong, —
He would live calmly, usefully, and long,
Plough earth, sow corn, make life a pastoral song,
So in his love he dreamed, — stirred by no fear
That life was useless, unless age and youth....
And life made slave of him....Meanwhile the earth —
Still through the starlight danced her endless song....
Life's cry she heard not; knew not right or wrong....

Not once but three times a benedict,
Experienced Jim-Aiken would reject
Reluctantly, the servitude
Of husbandry and fatherhood
To "follow a star", — flickering but long-pursued.
I have quoted at such length from Youth,
Not for its excellence as a poem but for its truth.
For all its high color, Aiken's portrait of Jim
Seems, rather, a convincing likeness of him.

• • •

The last poems in Earth Triumphant attest
The origin and significance of a pact
Conceived, at first, with light hearted wit,
(A slight disguise barely concealing it,
A later poem, "Changing Mind", clearly revealing it);
Whereby Eliot and Aiken interfuse
Identities so completely,
Effect their merger so discreetly,
That few will guess a riddle, much less a contract.

"Innocence" contrasts Aiken-Allegro's youth
With Eliot-Penseroso's "Sophistication":
        Then to his <u>soul</u>, <u>a</u> <u>twilight</u> <u>room</u>,
        Returning, he would sit in gloom;...
        Through this <u>grey spirit's twilight air</u>
        I think there often rose a prayer...
        To his own soul, perhaps addressed;...
        To give him life, with bliss and pain,
        To make new blood beat in old scars...

        But who has seen truth through his brain
        Hardly shall he return again
        To live in senses, nothing more;
        A <u>hollow sea-shell flung ashore</u>,
        Life has no use for him, nor sings
        Her warm song in him; he is sped;
        He hears the <u>lost sea's murmurings,</u>
        A ghost <u>wind roaring through his head</u>...
        He dreams, but cannot hate or love....

        A long while he had hoped, I think
        That some day he might deeply drink
        <u>Love from a woman's living mouth</u>
        And so put end to this long drought....
        And hungered for his miracle;
        Alas, he knew this sham too well...
        All magic but illusion is....
        He saw too keenly, drove away
        This magic by the light of day...

Wearily, year by year, he went
To theatre, cinematograph,
That haply he might cry or laugh,
Or swiftly taken unaware
Feel a cold horror creep his hair....
Often he smiled his cynic smile
But felt well-paid if every while
Suddenly came a gust of grief
Shaking his soul's trees ....

In "Laughter: Youth Speaks to His Own Old Age",
Aiken adopts a different device
To contrast Eliot's monastic mood,
Deficiency of blood, with his own lustihood.
But to detect addressee as adversary
One need only thumb Eliot's poetry,
All the underlined phrases are there —
In "Gerontion"; "Ash Wednesday"; "Marina";
"Usk" — indeed, everywhere:

(Particularly, in "Usk" where one may find
Such lines felicitously combined
With scene and song from an old play by Peele;
    ...do not spell
      Old enchantments. Let them sleep,
      Gently dip, but not too deep...
In reading "Cape Ann",
One might do well to rescan
Jim's musing about the sea-gulls.)...

• • •

You, whom these eyes, no longer mine,
Shall see the mirror's flash and shine…
All the grey shipwreck of this me…
You word that's uttered, you tune that's played,
You body shrunken, you soul decayed,
You heart that whispers but cannot sing…
Here is my hand upon your hand,
A stronger grip than yours can stand
Here are my words, so cruelly true,…

And because you are feeble, a crawling thing,
Walking by walls to hold and cling,
With terror of darkness on your breath,
And terror lest you be dead, with death:
Catching perhaps at straws of faith,
Drunk with religion in hope to drown
These maddening truths that will not down,
Clutching philosophy's vapid wraith,
Here is my perfect scorn for you.…

However weak, life fends for self, —
Thus you, old ghost! You shuffling trimer!…
Poor soul! Go, make your peace with death,
And warm your heart with a shibboleth.
… But here's my laughing dirk,
Here I have snared you, all complete,
Your pitiful pale hands, struggling feet;
If you breathe poison on my art,
Here is my poniard, here your heart!…

• • •

So Aiken taunts Eliot — effeminate,
Impotent and dessicate,
Telling his beads amidst the gloom,
In his chill, dank cell-like room,
Mumbling ancient prayers and spells
In vain hope to penetrate
That inmost shrine where dwells
Invisible, impalpable, the Ultimate,
Veiled, unapproachable — Absolute.

Natural, supernatural, masculine, feminine,
Animal, human, or divine —
Each would pursue
In his own way, his private quest.
Let the world pronounce that poet best
Who achieved, at the last,
The greatest acclaim,
Acknowledged success,
World-shaking fame.

• • •

The bond was signed; the race began;
Work succeeded work.
The first remained American,
Professing Freud and pragmatism;
The second became High Anglican;
Espousing the program of L'Action
Francaise — "cosmic" or, at least, cosmopolitan —
To restore the bulwark and bastion
Of authority and Dogmatism.

The American shifted from mate to mate;
Eliot, though married, remained celibate;
Self-proclaimed "Classicist", Royalist, High Churchman,
Renounced his American birthright to become
A Tory Englishman, expert in polemics;
Shrewdly exploiting his martyrdom —
Backed by Government, Church, Academics —
Basking in honor, boredom, glory
Beloved of Royalty, Aristocracy, and Military.

• • •

From tentative beginnings and private purposes
In their youthful pact and earliest verses,
The pair progressed to their impressive roles
In a global cult, largely of E. Pound's invention.
"In lieu of a viable tradition", — he said,
"Better mendacities than the classics in paraphrase"
Translating Aiken-Jones and Eliot-Smith
Into major gods in a sacred myth,
Based on the Egyptian <u>Book</u> <u>of</u> <u>the</u> <u>Dead</u>.

After Frazer, of course, but reinterpreted
By Henri Frankfort and, with the help of his wife,
Given new circulation and life.
Viewed among much else, as a fertility rite,
With Osiris-Aiken as the buried god,
It acquired allegorical verisimilitude
When Pound, as the murderer Set, redistributed
Fragments of Aiken's work, already planted
In the <u>Waste</u> <u>Land</u> and elsewhere, as previously indicated.

After a process minutely described
In Aiken's poem, "A Changing Mind",
Where the poet is "separated out" upon a table
(His work, that is, syllable by syllable),
And buried like the flesh of Osiris,
In the voice and work of the other,
Left for the goddess Isis to recover,
And a tardy world
To discover.

In the Preface to that poem,
Aiken confesses himself a "willing participant" —
To some extent, even the instigator
Of the action — seeing himself "resolved
Into his constituent particles",
As part of "the evolving consciousness of man",
He would make his "experience available
For the benefit of others",
Be the "servant example" of his lesser "brothers".

• • •

Frankfort, in his various works,
Explains how the Dead
Travel the "cosmic circuit",
"Rolled round", as Wordworth said,
"With rocks and stones and trees;"
So it is with "cult initiates"
Who, still in their mortal states,
"Mingle with the Living" in the "worst of all ages",
According to the poet, William Butler Yeats.

In her essay, "Piers Plowman and the Modern Waste Land",
The erudite Christine Brooke-Rose agrees
With the view that the "Pound Industry" is a "conspiracy"—
Or series of such. "Pound, no less than Langland", she says,
Has kept textual scholars and elucidators at work:
If some of Pound's allusions are even more recondite,
He is alive to answer questions, and, in "humorous" delight,
Boast of the invention of a god (or goddess)
Scholars, as yet, have been unable to trace.

Eliot plays a royal role as the sun-god, Amon-Ra
(Later, to be assimilated with a sniggering Pound,
As a "sky-goddess", the compound-complex
"Princess Ra-Set", with reference to Set's redemption
And Eliot's ambiguous sex.)
The cult is kept alive by drastic medication,
Unremitting artificial respiration,
Fervent disciples, desperate remedies,
And bare-faced falsification.

• • •

Book following book, Aiken's prose —
Novels, stories, reviews — disclose
The progress of their plot in cryptogram and code,
As also his poetry — in "symphony", "verse-legend", "prelude",
With the late culmination of all in the autobiography, Ushant.
(Jasper Amen in King Coffin is a trial-portrait
Of Eliot-Nietzsche; as also Hay-Lawrence plus Cynthia-saint,
(The stained-glass widow), in Blue Voyage — and Demarest —
Of Aiken, the sacrificed god, with a crucified pig for surrogate.)

• • •

As early as "Ash Wednesday", Eliot proclaimed
An end to the collaboration,
Speaking sometimes in the person of Aiken,
As in Part II, where the leopards "have fed to satiety"
        On my legs my heart my liver and that which has been contained
        In the hollow round of my skull...that
        Which had been contained
        In the bones (which were already dry) said chirping;
        We shine with brightness. And I who am dissembled

        Proffer my deeds to oblivion, and my love
        To the posterity of the desert and the fruit of the gourd...
        It is this which recovers
        My guts the strings of my eyes and the indigestible portions
        Which the leopards reject...
        Let the whiteness of bones atone to forgetfulness.
        There is no life in them...
        Under a juniper-tree the bones sang, scattered and shining
        We are glad to be scattered, we did little good to each other...

        Forgetting themselves and each other, united
        In the quiet of the desert. This is the land which ye
        Shall divide by lot. And neither division nor unity
        Matters. This is the land. We have our inheritance...
        The new year's walk, restoring
        Through a bright cloud of tears, the years, restoring
        With a new verse the ancient rhyme. Redeem...
        The unread vision in the higher dream
        While jewelled unicorns draw by the gilded hearse...

Or again in Part IV, no less cryptically;

> The silent sister veiled in white and blue
> Between the yews, behind the garden god,
> Whose flute is breathless, bent her head and signed
> But spake no word...
> But the fountain sprang up and the bird sang down
> Redeem the time, redeem the dream
> The token of the word unheard, unspoken
> Till the wind shake a thousand whispers from the yew...
> And after this our exile

. . .

At the conclusion of the famous passage in "Little Gidding",
The "familiar compound ghost" is allowed
To present his defense,
Not unaccompanied by misgivings,
Perhaps, even, by apology and regret,
As he reviews the gifts reserved for age:
> These things have served their purpose: let them be...
> Last season's fruit is eaten
> And the fullfed beast shall kick the empty pail....

> Since our concern was speech, and speech impelled us
> To purify the dialect of the tribe
> And urge the mind to aftersight and foresight,
> Let me disclose to gifts reserved for age
> To set a crown upon your lifetime's effort.
> First, the cold friction of expiring sense
> Without enchantment, offering no promise
> But bitter tastelessness of shadow fruit
> As body and soul begin to fall asunder.

Second, the conscious impotence of rage
    At human folly, and the laceration
    Of laughter at what ceases to amuse.
And last, the rending pain of re-enactment
    Of all that you have done, and been; the shame
    Of motives late revealed, and the awareness
Of things ill done and done to others' harm
    Which once you took for exercise of virtue.
    Then fools' approval stings, and honour stains.

• • • •

Pound's participation is acknowledged in "The Dry Salvages"
("Les Trois Sauvages") footnote, as earlier in "The Journey of the
Magi";

Then at dawn we came down to a temperate valley,
Wet, below the snow line, smelling of vegetation;
With a running stream and water-mill beating the darkness,
And three trees on the low sky,
And an old white horse galloped away in the meadow.
Then we came to a tavern with vine-leaves over the lintel,
Six hands at an open door dicing for pieces of silver,
And feet kicking the empty wine-skins...

---

1 (The Dry Salvages — presumably les trois sauvages — is a small group of rocks, with a beacon, off the N.E. coast of Cape Ann, Massachusetts. Salvage is pronounced to rhyme with assuages. Groaner: a whistling buoy.) Eliot's Notes.

And arrived at evening......

And in these incantatory lines in <u>The</u> <u>Family</u> <u>Reunion:</u>

> The eye is on this house.
> The eye covers it
> There are three together
> > May the three be separated
> > May the knot that was tied
> > Become unknotted
> > May the crossed bones
> > In the filled-up well
>
> Be at last straightened
> May the weasel and the otter
> Be about their proper business
> The eye of the day time
> And the eye of the night time
> Be diverted from this house
> Till the knot is unknotted
> The crossed is uncrossed
> And the crooked is made straight.

• • •

Imagination — creation — creativity —
Have we an answer to the mystery?
Is it a hoax to be exposed then?
A joke to be played upon lesser men
For the wry pleasure of a privileged few?
"Who lives, who dies?" the poet Aiken cries
At the close of one of his "symphonies",
"Who knows the secret of immortal springs"...
"We hold them all, they walk our dreams forever,

"Nothing perishes in that haunted air,
Nothing but is immortal there,
And we ourselves, dying with all our worlds
Will only pass this ghostly portal
Into another's dream, and so live on
Through dream to dream immortal."
Not the Muses but the mother of them all
Mnemosyne, would seem the answer —— and Memory
Is, for the poet, mainly verbal.

• • •

Memory, long-submerged, unconscious even,
Accounts for the "discovery"
In 1949 which constitutes the basis of my thesis.
A middle-aged English teacher,
A widow with a son to be educated,
Not too happily situated,
In an old-fashioned "teachers' college"
In a small southwestern town,
Overworked and, as folk-say has it, "beaten down",

I deplored the "moderns" of Eliot-Pound persuasion,
Although helpless to stem the invasion
Of what the authorities called "progressive innovation,"
And I, only Babel, as compounded by the "New Criticism",
I was teaching a course called "The Study of Poetry"
And so "had to" read them with whatever revulsion,
I was under no compulsion
To read Ezra Pound, but T.S. Eliot
Was "required" by the text and, therefore, a "must".

Reading Eliot's first lyric in "Landscape",
Did I hear an echo of Milne's verses:
     Anne, Anne walking with her man…
          Brown head, gold head, down among the buttercups….
In Eliot's "Golden Head, Crimson Head"?
It amused me to think so.
Remembering his comments upon other experiences
Of sex in childhood; Dante's first sight
Of Beatrice; his own anecdotal poem in French.

"Dans le Restaurant", where the patron
Receiving the unwelcome confidence of the waiter,
Recognizes the defeat and lust of the latter,
With anger and disgust, as his own.
These random reflections combined
Into vague formulation of a satirical essay,
Dante, Eliot, Christopher Robin,
And the Auditory Imagination,
With Edmund Wilson and the New Yorker in mind.

• • •

Reading Eliot, in this mood, perhaps more
Attentively than before,
I was struck by the passage numbered Four
In the first of the Quartets, "Burnt Norton" —
In the underlying pattern of the first lines
I had already noted
The resemblance to an anonymous "nonsense" poem,
Much discussed and quoted
In various textbook anthologies:

     "The bailey beareth the bell away,
     The lily, the rose, the rose I lay—"

A Familiar Compound Ghost Reconstituted

The concluding six lines, I was suddenly convinced,
I had read before in a different context. Where?
In an effort so intense as too be almost trance,
I wrenched from my subconscious memory
An all but forgotten phrase of my youth,
When "The Morning Song of Senlin" in some anthology,
Had awakened in me, an ecstasy
Which led to the baffled pursuit of the idol —
The god — who had created this miracle.

• • •

What was she like — that young girl
Awakened by "The Morning Song of Senlin"
Brought alive into a world
Of music, of color, of vision? —
(She who had hitherto only "existed")
Made "happily consscious" of her universe;
Given words to describe it;
Live in it; possess it;
Make it her own?

Like a reed in water
Dipping and swaying;
Bending with the wind,
To be swiftly taken,
Washed under —
To rise again shaken;
Lifting, submerging, drifting;
Passive, unconscious, loath
To awaken.

What was she like — that young girl?
That <u>tabula</u> not quite <u>rasa</u>?
Palimpsest, rather, cut deeply,
Scarred with sensation, emotion —
Invisible wounds, everlasting —
Summoned in trance; remembered in dream —
As half a life-time later occurred,
When reading Eliot, she heard
Aiken's voice — and memory stirred.

• • •

"It is morning, Senlin says, and in the morning
When the light drips through the shutters like dew
I arise, I face the sunrise,
And do the things my fathers learned to do.
Stars in the purple dusk above the roof-tops
Pale in a saffron mist and seem to die,
And I myself on a swiftly tilting planet
Stand before a glass and tie my tie...
Upright and firm I stand on a star unstable —

"It is morning. I stand by the mirror
And surprise my soul once more...
While waves far off in a pale rose twilight
Crash on a coral shore....
The green earth tilts through a sphere of air
And bathes in a flame of space
There are houses hanging above the stars
And stars hung under a sea...
And a sun far off in a shell of silence...

"Dapples my walls for me.
Time is a wind, says Senlin: Time, like music,
Blows over us its mournful beauty, passes,
And leaves behind a shadowy recollection —
A helpless gesture of mist above the grasses....
Vine leaves tap at my window,
Dew-drops sing to the garden stones,
The robin chirps in the chinaberry tree,
Repeating three clear tones....

"It is morning. I awake from a bed of silence
Shining I rise from the starless waters of sleep.
The walls are about me still as in the evening,
I am the same, and the same name still I keep.
The earth revolves with me, yet makes no motion....
The blue air rushes above my ceiling,
There are suns beneath my floor....
It is morning, Senlin says, I ascend from darkness
And depart on the winds of space for I know not where....

• • •

"I stepped from a cloud, he says, as evening fell;
I walked on the sound of a bell...
Has no one, in a great autumnal forest,
When the wind bares the trees,
Heard the sad horn of Senlin slowly blown?...
Perhaps I came alone on a snow-white horse, —
Riding alone from the deep-starred night.
Perhaps I came on a ship whose sails were music...

"Senlin, walking before us in sunlight...
Regards white horses drawing a small white hearse
'Is it my childhood there,' he asks
Sealed in a hearse and hurrying by?[1]
'Nevertheless, I know this well
Bury it deep and toll a bell,
Bury it under land or sea,
You cannot bury it save in me,'...
The white spokes dazzle and turn....

"Death himself in the rain...death himself...
Death himself in the dusk, gathering lilacs,
Breaking a white-flashed bough...
I do not see him, but I see the lilacs fall...
The leaves are tossed and tremble where he plunges among them,
And I hear the sound of his breath,
Sharp and whistling, the rhythm of death.
We are the grains of sand
Who thought ourselves immortal...."

• • •

In the "Preface" previous referred to,
Aiken is at pains to differentiate
That poem from Senlin; "If Senlin:A Biography
May be said to provide the generic 'I'
That underlines The Divine Pilgrim, the block unit
Of human reference, "Changing Mind"
Might be called the specific 'I' at a specific moment
In its experience, in a specific predicament...
Wholly anonymous and perhaps with reason."

---

[1] I was startled in reading a few years ago, The Poems and Plays of T.S. Eliot by Professor Grover Smith, in the section "Notes and References to Pages 145-152" on page 315, note 30, the following personal reference: Aiken told me in 1949 that the resemblance to "Ash Wednesday" had previously been noticed by Mrs. E. F. Piper.

"Perhaps with reason", indeed! That specific "I"
Inherits not only "the basic unconscious memory"
Of Senlin"—with which I had so naturally "identified",
But also the situation of that highly complex
"Neurotic artist", Conrad Aiken, with whom
(As further reading in his work
Unhappily convinced me), I had little in common —
Or could have — or only as inheritor of "racial memories",
And through them, of "deeper instinctual responses".

● ● ● ●

And yet, I would not be ungrateful,
I had heard him speak and his voice would not be forgotten...
Literature is like a vast chorus,
Receding backward in time,
Expanding in space. One does not <u>see</u> print;
One <u>hears</u> voices – passionate, lyrical,
Raucous, sublime. One's own voice blends
With the singing. Is this Aiken's meaning?
Is this what the poet intends?

● ● ●

I re-read with care my own neglected
Copies of early books by Aiken,
And, thought I did not find the passage
I though the source of Eliot's lines:
> Will the sunflower turn to us,
> Will the clematis....
I recalled two rhymes from it—
"The holly-hocks and the four o'clocks"
And knew that I could not be mistaken.

• • •

I boldly wrote Aiken, himself, to say
That I had resolved the poets' "enigma"
(Which, at that date, was a good deal less than true!)
And received an air mail reply,
Expressing great "excitement" and interest, and presently,
Endorsement of my project of a book,
Recommending that I send it to Philip Vaudrin of the Oxford Press,
And granting <u>carte</u> <u>blanche</u> for quotation, —
To which Eliot, later, added permission, subject to his inspection.

• • •

My "teaching load" was five undergraduate classes,
Distributed throughout a six-day week
In such a way, as to leave me "free"
For a class of out-of-town teachers,
From ten to one on Saturday;
That is, my campus classes
Met on "T days" at eight and nine.
I taught Freshman Composition; World Literature;
"Poetry", and English Literature Survey.

Mother Hubbard's cupboard was hardly more bare
Than our library—one book by Aiken was all it afforded.
Our then "Head" lacked a Ph.D.,
And reluctant to engage a possible rival,
Refused my request for even a summer-term leave,
It was up to me strictly; I was on my own:
To order Aiken's books, seek typists,
And above all, to find time
To do what required to be done.

I think, "How different things are today!"
And then question, "Are they?"
Much lip-service is paid "research",
But what imports is, in fact, "publication"—
Meaning "public relations". Faculty are allowed to pursue
"Approved" projects; money flows fairly freely
For books, clerical help, travel expenses.
But would my thesis find more favor now?
I very much doubt it. Not really!

• • •

Beginning per force, <u>in</u> <u>medias</u> <u>res</u>,
I was only gradually able to trace
The plot back to its primary source,
Through later works to the earliest verse,
By that time, the title had changed
From <u>Eliot</u>, <u>Aiken</u>, <u>and</u> <u>The</u> <u>Auditory</u> <u>Imagination</u>
To <u>A</u> <u>Familiar</u> <u>Compound</u> <u>Ghost</u>, though Aiken demurred.
I had divined their intimate relation
But was unprepared for the revelation

That what I had supposed a more-or-less innocent game
Was, in the context, rather closer to treason.
In any case, the controversy over the Bollingen Award
To Ezra Pound had begun
And Aiken, hastily recanting, withdrew,
Though not before I had conceived it my duty
To make my discoveries known
To responsible scholars and had diffidently begun
By inditing a long naïve letter

To F.S.C. Northrop, whose <u>The</u> <u>Meeting</u> <u>of</u> <u>East</u> <u>and</u> <u>West</u>
Had won my respect and admiration,
I reported my discoveries, speculation,
Suspicions, receiving a reply from his secretary,
Saying that Mr. Northrop was "out of the country",
By that time, Hillyer's articles in <u>The</u> <u>Saturday</u> <u>Review</u>
Had corroborated what I already knew,
And I wrote that the letter be forwarded to him,
Sending a duplicate to the editor, absent, too.

Hillyer replied at once, courteously
Assuring me that he did not "deem" me "a crank",
But that the "ramifications of this thing"
Were beyond "the powers of any one man—
Or woman"—to expose, urging me to "leave it alone",
To "put my material in trustworthy hands",
And "turn my attention to happier things"—
"We are all required to fight evil", he said, "up to,
But not beyond, our strength". By then,

The Fellows of the Library of Congress
And their friends
Were everywhere up in arms,
Hillyer under brutal attack;
All "true lovers of Art, Literature and Culture",
Rallying to slogans of "Freedom of Speech and of the Arts".
The Fascists had made good, I thought, their boasts
Of reprisal and triumph! Truth and Justice
Were forever—and irretrievably—lost.

Distraught, ill, despairing, I swallowed sleeping pills
And turned on the gas in my bathroom.
I was not, like Celia Coplestone, crucified near ant hills,
In darkest Kinkaja nor, like the kitten
In Aiken's "Hello, Tib!", swept beneath wheels
Of an onrushing train. My "ordeal"
Was not that of "Miss X" in Lord Russell's allegory.
Yet, a fate worse than death? Not quite, perhaps,
But horror enough—and nearly.

I had never thought the world good
Or life easy but I had not known
What I had now experienced, been shown:
That <u>nothing was what it appeared</u>;
That the world I supposed we all shared
Was a <u>sham</u> and <u>a snare</u> <u>no</u> <u>one</u> <u>dared</u>
To doubt — much less expose what it was —
Even <u>if</u> <u>he</u> <u>saw</u> <u>and</u> <u>knew</u> — <u>and</u> <u>very</u> <u>few</u>
Did. It was certain that I never could.

Perhaps it was best that I should
Follow Hillyer's advice and not try.
But where were the trustworthy hands
Wherein I should place my aborted ms..
<u>A</u> <u>Familiar</u> <u>Compound</u> <u>Ghost</u>.
And the whole sorry record
Of my fatal quest
With its consequences
To my life, mind and senses?

• • •

The scholars I approached,
If kindly, were evasive;
Some few annoyed and abrasive;
The thesis was "absurd on the face of it",
The sort of thing a flighty woman — no scholar —
Would "dream up"— become possessed by.
The subject, unfortunately broached,
Must be firmly, if politely, dismissed;
The thesis summarily scotched.

• • •

With no one anywhere to depend on,
By 1952 I resolved to abandon
The useless search and carry
My "materials", as Hillyer called them,
To the Iowa Authors' Room
In the State University of Iowa Library
Where I had long before been invited to place
Any writing, published or unpublished,
My husband's or my own, that I cared to,

I made the trip between the end
Of summer school and the next fall term,
To find only a skeleton library staff —
No one interested at all in my mission.
At last, a man concerned with "acquisition"
In a hurry to depart on vacation,
"Accepted" a selection
From my husband's ballad collection
For circulation, and my packets to await further direction

• • •

Between 1952 and 1973
When the world of my past was reopened for me
By a request for data about the incumbency
Of my husband as English professor
At the University of Iowa and as sponsor
Of "creative writing" before the establishment
Of the famous "Iowa Workshop", for a "history"
Designed to glorify
That institution — its forebears and progeny.

I had resumed and pursued
Class room teaching, tamed and subdued,
Knowing I should never be able
To outlive the stigma attached to my "unstable"
Behavior, in the "break-down" of '49;
Desiring only to escape attention,
Never daring to speak of promotion;
Despairing, resigned, prone
To self-abasement, less than half-alive.

• • •

Grateful, at last, to be retired,
I should never again have aspired
To action on the world scene.
At first I thought to ignore the request
For aid. The woman addressed—
The time they referred to—were dead;
If they had ever been, could not be resurrected.
I was old, ill, and too tired
To summon the energy required.

Let them say what they chose—
Still some spark must have burned in the ashes,
Some flicker emerged into flame,
For I finally wrote—and at some length.[1]
I paid my respects to Norman Foerster
And his Irving Babbitt regime,
As expounded by Austin Warren in an essay,
"The New Humanism Twenty Years After",
Published in Volume I of the <u>Modern</u> <u>Age</u>
Then sub-titled: <u>A</u> <u>Conservative</u> <u>Review.</u>

• • • •

We suffered through nine years of it ——
The machinations, manipulations, "finesse" ——
Until in 1939, my husband's untimely death
Forced a decision upon me;
To suppress hesitation and scruples
And submit my book of verses
As "partial fulfillment" of requirements for the Ph.D.—
(The first such thesis, as I know now, and then believed),
Dedicated to my husband— and reluctantly received ——

Or so I must suppose, since no public mention
Has ever been made of it,
The prospects of a teaching position
For a woman like me, in the late years of the Depression
Were sufficiently grim, but such was my dread
And loathing of the stifling, conspiratorial air
That though I was offered a position of sorts,
My only thought was escape,
And I recklessly fled.

---

[1] See <u>Edwin Ford Piper and the Iowa Workshop: A Memoir</u>

• • •

It was to be more than twenty years,
When I had, at last, retired
Before I inquired
And learned that my "materials"
Had disappeared.
How and why I have never heard,
But in view of all that had occurred,
I have stoutly averred:
"That 'compound ghost' must be disinterred."

Holocausts, treasons, cold war intervene —
But when survivors are counted
"Modern" poets loom large on the scene,
(Though Pound may be somewhat discounted).
True, Isis had discovered the bones
Of Osiris. Jones-Smith or Smith-Jones
Had discarded those avatars;
Osiris-Aiken, the resurrected god,
Resumed his career undaunted.

• • • •

It was 1973 when I delivered my "bomb threat"
As a challenge to old men still living —
Poets who concurred
In the "take-over" — furthered
The "revolution of the word"
For purposes of their own;
Satirists, double-agents, wits —
To acknowledge their misdeeds
Before death — to "come clean".

There have been no explosions;
I have heard no stampedes —
No rush for absolution.
The world proceeds
As before — but not I!
I am alive again! Before I die
I shall, at last,
Have reconstituted the "compound ghost";
Validated my "Doctor of Letters" degree.[1]

---

[1] See <u>The University of Iowa's Writer's Workshop: A Reminiscence</u>.